The Four
Fundamental
Questions

The Four Fundamental Questions

Talks and essays about
human experience and
the actual practice
of an Enlightened Way of Life

by Da Free John

The Dawn Horse Press
Clearlake Highlands, California

First edition January 1980
Printed in the United States of America
International Standard Book Number
        paper 0-913922-49-8
Library of Congress Catalog Card Number
        79-92923

Produced by Vision Mound Ceremony
in cooperation with
The Dawn Horse Press

Vision Mound Ceremony

Contents

The fundamental questions of this life are too urgent for us to wait for the perfection of acquired knowledge, and they are too important for us to "answer" with conventional belief.

Da Free John
The Enlightenment of the Whole Body

"Availability Land" and Certain Death versus the Way of Enlightened Happiness

by Saniel Bonder

I f you were told that you have five minutes left to live, what would you do? What would you think? How would you feel?

None of us likes to consider this prospect. No one is interested in actually passing into the mystery that is beyond this life. No one is merely amused or enthusiastically intrigued by that prospect! Yet we all must die someday. Everyone who has ever lived has died. Everyone! This is certainly a sobering, if not terrifying, realization. We appear in this life without a clue to our origins, with no forewarning, having made no conscious choice of which we are even vaguely aware. As we grow, we begin to recognize all the alternatives of experience and knowledge that confront us. Da Free John has remarked that we tend to view the world as an "Availability Land." Every kind of experience is available, like many flavors of ice cream, and we spend our lifetime choosing to satisfy ourselves with sex and knowledge, food and power, the mundane pleasures of family life and the esoteric adventures of space exploration or mystical experience. We think Truth and happiness can be found in our own brains—or perhaps even in our underwear!—until we seriously confront our inevitable death.

Billions of men and women have played in "Availability Land" in this life, and then they have all died. Not a single one of them to date has returned to tell us convincingly and conclusively of his or her immortality. Not one. The great passage of death still mystifies and terrifies the living, no matter what we hope or believe. A few may catch glimmers of survival beyond death, which inspire them to launch crusades to convince others of our ultimate immortality. However, whatever else may be said and known, there is a part of every human being that is dramatically and often gruesomely mortal—and those who truly feel this mortality cannot be consoled by promises, hopes, or even apparitions of the great beyond.

No amount or kind of information or experience will save you, me, or anyone else from pain, suffering, and death, or make us wise in the midst of pleasures that inevitably pass. Many of you who read this book will already have had many kinds of mystical, yogic, visionary, and transcendental experience. On the other hand, many—perhaps the same people—will also have exploited the more ordinary distractions such as eating, drinking, drug-taking, and sexing, self-help and psychological analysis, ordinary religious belief and churchgoing, and all the possibilities for fame and success in the arenas of money, power, the arts, politics, and the like. What has any experience accomplished for you? No experience or achievement, high or low, makes us more fit to love and be continually happy in this bewildering life. We have read and seen and heard and felt and known many, many things—yet we are still only preparing to confront the fundamental fact of our very existence in the world. Witness our response to the threat of death. We do not understand death. We are still clinging to our lives, trying to survive and succeed. Death terrifies us! Mortal fear has a way of revealing how superficial are all our beliefs, our knowledge, our religion, our business, our politics, our yoga, our experience.

The common mood of people, young or old, who confront the facts of bodily existence and death is despair. "Availability Land" no longer attracts and consoles—its promise of unending experience appears boring, repetitive, and devoid of any lasting pleasure or happiness. We thus feel or recognize the limits and suffering inherent in mere experience, and we begin spontaneously to conceive and consider the fundamental questions of our existence itself. Where are we? What are we? How did all this come to be? What is our Source, and what is our relationship to It?

In this book such fundamental questions are phrased for us by a great man of Wisdom, Da Free John. In this book we are not merely given the "answers" to life's great questions. This book is a consideration, a process of self-examination that you may engage by entertaining the questions Da Free John puts to you. The consideration in itself will not

"Enlighten" you, nor is it intended to console or fascinate you or arouse your interest in self-improvement, like so many of the enlightenment seminars, salvation techniques, and self-help programs that are offered all over the world today. However, if you consider these questions carefully and continually, they will inevitably <u>lead</u> you to take up a Way of life that is essentially or in principle enlightened, happy, and free. That Way will not be easy or quick. You still must struggle creatively with the conditions of your own living, and you must still deal with your own death. But you will perhaps realize a new relationship to the affairs of life and death—a disposition of ecstasy, love, boundless joy, and the wisdom that surpasses mere knowing.

The "four fundamental questions" presented here emerged from the considerations of a living Spiritual Teacher, Da Free John, who was born and lives in the West, with those who practice the Way of Life that he Teaches. Many hundreds of people have come to him since he began to teach in 1972, two years after his own perfect realization of spiritual Enlightenment. They have found Da Free John to be a man of great Wisdom and spiritual Power, capable of awakening the undeniable intuition of the Divine in those who see him and hear his Teaching. We will tell you more about Da Free John and his work in the world in Part II of this book, after you have passed through the considerations or questions he offers.

Now, however, if it has become obvious to you again (for we always feel it beneath our casual pretenses) that death is inevitable and that the suffering we can realize in this life and in death is far more profound and lasting than the pleasure we may acquire through experience in any moment—then read on to learn of the way whereby we may become absolutely happy even while alive, and also absolutely free of naive illusions about life, death, and all possible experience.

Saniel Bonder
Talking God Seminary
Clearlake Highlands, CA

PART I

The Fundamental Questions That Inevitably Lead to an Enlightened Way of Life

CHAPTER 1

Are You the One Who Is Living You Now?

A talk by Da Free John

I

DA FREE JOHN: What are the questions that if answered truly would Enlighten you and would lead you to practice the Way of Truth? Obviously you have never asked yourself these questions, or you would be totally transformed by now! You can ask many useful questions that might lead you to consider or think about the Way, but what questions would make the practice of real or spiritual life inevitable if you were to answer them fully?

The first question must necessarily draw your attention to the fact that the Condition in which you actually exist is entirely different from the condition you are presuming in this moment. Because you are struggling to survive as yourself, you have endless desires, numberless goals, and countless forms of knowledge and self-involvement that occupy your energy and attention. Having presented yourself as such a struggling one, then, you must first ask yourself this question: **Are you the one who is living you now?** Are you personally responsible for your existence?

You are involved, you see, in a complex life that ultimately refers to yourself in very practical terms now and in every moment. Nevertheless, are you— that one who is right here and can respond to my questions right now—are you the one who is living you at this moment? Or is your living merely happening? Are you accomplishing your present living any more than you did your birth? You are struggling for survival, dominance, knowledge, longevity, immortality, pleasure, and happiness. Are <u>you</u> the essential or primary subject of your own existence? Are you living yourself and creating yourself? Are you?

I can enlarge upon the first question, then, and ask you: Are you, or any collection of others like you, living the <u>world</u> at this moment? Are you who respond to my question now existing as the world at the present time? Are you living it? Are you the One enlivening it and creating its motion? Are you the One Who is living and breathing those around you? Are you digesting their food or pumping their blood? Are you? You say no. Well, then, are you profoundly aware that you are not that One? Merely to consider and answer these questions, you see, will almost instantly reveal to you that some One, some Thing, some Power, is existing as and enlivening the world. We cannot conceive of it. Except for our limited finding out or knowing about things, we are in a state of complete Ignorance, or Mystery.

In Divine Ignorance you recognize that you are not living yourself. You depend entirely on a Life-Process for which you bear not even the remotest responsibility. You are somehow the effect of that Process. You notice it, you cooperate with it, and you are implicated in it, but you are not independently responsible for it.

Someone other than the "you" who responds to my question, some One, some Power, some Being, is being you right now. That One is responsible for you, for living you and for bringing you into existence.

Everyone that I ask must confess that he is not living himself or the world, nor does he bring himself or the world or anything whatsoever into being at any time. Even your own thoughts are a Mystery to you. You do not know what a thought is, do you? You are somehow implicated in thoughts but you do not know what thought is. You do not, ultimately, create thought. You are associated somehow or other with the process of thought, just as you are somehow defined by the whole body-mind, but you are not the One Who is presently living and being that body-mind. Nor are you the One Who brought it into being twenty, thirty, forty, fifty or more years ago.

Not only did you not give yourself birth, but also you are not presently being yourself. The One Who created you, that Dimension of existence, includes you; it is living and being you at this moment. That One is also the only One Who can tell me that He—or She—is you. Who else could be you but the One

14

Who is existing as you, the One Who brings you into being, the One in Whom you are arising, changing, and, even now, disintegrating and dying? You are not living yourself nor any other thing. Nor are you even able to confess that you are living. You are <u>lived</u>, but you are not living. You are somehow the mechanical implication or effect of this existing, living process; and you are experientially always differentiated from that process and not responsible for it.

II

DA FREE JOHN: The second question is not "<u>Who</u> is living you?" We are in a condition of Ignorance, or Mystery, relative to the Identity of the One Who is living us. Our realization of the One Who lives us is not ultimately an answer to a question—it transcends knowledge. You are not the One Who is living you, breathing your breath, pounding your heart, animating you altogether at present. Obviously you are being lived. Obviously all of this world is spontaneously arising. Something or Someone is responsible for manifest existence, but it is not you. You are the independent one who is struggling to conquer and survive.

Since you cannot affirm that you are the One living as yourself or as anything whatsoever, what kind of relationship do you presume to have with whatever It is that <u>is</u> living you? What kind of moment to moment relationship do you presume to have with your actual Existence, with the ultimate Being, with Life, with God? The second fundamental question, then, following upon your answer to the first, is: **"What is your relationship to that One?"**

You all have a strange and neurotic relationship, I would say, to the Process in which you are arising. You act as if you could say yes to my first question, as if you were the Creator and Subject altogether of manifest experience, of your birth, and of the appearance of anything at all and everything altogether. You act as if you were the Subject of experience, as if you were living as everything, as if you were the Ultimate Knower, as if you were in the position of ultimate power. Yet at the same time you are struggling to survive.

You act as if, as a result of serious consideration, you had discovered that you are omnipresent, immortal, all-powerful, responsible for your own existence. In fact you are not. You are a zero in the midst of all of this! You know nothing about even this present moment of experience. Starting from zero, you hope to accumulate knowledge and power and, ultimately, immortality in order to glamorize and pleasure yourself. Yet you are not the One Who is living any of this at all. You are not profoundly involved in breathing yourself right now, are you? The breathing is happening. Even if, by investigating the brain, you could learn to control the process of the breath, you would not have brought it into being. You would simply have come to know about it to the extent that you could control some pulsation or other manifestation of the process of the breath in a single body. Such control is not tantamount to omniscience or absolute power. Can you, by taking thought, bring the breath of all beings to rest? No, you cannot. You can perhaps imagine doing a little medical investigation or yoga to the point of stopping your own breath or even your own heartbeat—there are people who can do these things— but you cannot even imagine terminating the breath of all beings.

You are a partial reflection of the totality of what is appearing in this moment. You are the body-mind referring to itself rather than to its Condition, its Being or Life. The usual "I" does not refer to anything great at all. When you use the word "I" you are not pointing toward God, toward the One Who lives and breathes as all beings. You are pointing to your own self, the body-mind. Still there must be Something or Someone in some dimension of existence that is living and breathing all beings. That Something is the Reality, Person, Power, Dimension, or Being that is actually being us at the present time. It is not only the God who created us, but It is also the One Who sustains us, because It is actually living and being us right now.

Thus, you can continue to play at finding out about the world through experiencing, knowing, increasing your grasp of information, mastering mechanical processes that are presently proceeding spontaneously and totally outside your realm of responsibility. You can even bring your bodily existence to rest without finding out how the body works—you can kill yourself, and, sure enough, the heartbeat will come to an end. However, that ending does not mean that you are the ultimately responsible party. You will have merely interrupted a process that would otherwise continue spontaneously.

Relative to the <u>existence</u> of anything, including yourself at this very moment, you are totally ignorant

and totally irresponsible. Anyone can observe this, you
see, whether an atheist, or a Roman Catholic, or a
Hindu mystic, or a Protestant believer, or a Jewish
rabbi. Anyone can consider this, and no one can
truthfully say to you "I am the One Who is being,
living, existing as me and as everything at this
moment." No "I" can tell you that, unless that "I"
begins to surrender and speak in ecstatic identity with
and praise of the Living God, Who creates and sustains
and ultimately brings to an end everything that exists.

III

DA FREE JOHN: What kind of relationship do
you presume to have in each moment to That
Which is living you, the One Who is you, Who is
living, breathing, creating, sustaining, and ultimately
even throwing you away, destroying you? You may be
an atheist or agnostic, angrily or coolly unwilling to
accept the arguments of conventional religion, but still
you must see that you are not the One Who is being
yourself, Who is living yourself or anything else. For
example, if oxygen alone is living and sustaining you,
you are therefore in a dependent position in relation to
oxygen, and you should be reflecting in your action a
consciousness of such dependence. If your existence
depends on nothing more than oxygen, you should be
surrendering to oxygen! To refuse to surrender to
oxygen—in other words, to forget your present
dependence on oxygen, having found yourself to exist
as a result of it—is to suffer. Recognize that you are

not living and breathing yourself, and then surrender to "oxygen"—or whatever that Power, Process, Being, or Force is that truly lives you.

You do not presently and always profoundly acknowledge that Being, that Force, that Presence. Quite the contrary, you are profoundly fixed in your independent self, and, therefore, in your refusal to acknowledge the very Being and Reality Who is Existing as everything. That refusal is obviously the problem. The problem is immediate. You are already existing in a wrong relationship to That which Exists, and that wrong disposition must be cured.

You are worried about death, yet the One Who is being you is the One Who will cause that death! Having opted to presume yourself to be "I," this limited self, this separate person or body-mind, you have assumed a neurotic or negative and contracted position. Your moment to moment existence is effectively a neurotic act of dissociation from the ultimate Reality (and even from all the relations of your "self"). If I ask you in this moment who you are, you will in one way or another define yourself as the body-mind. You are the one whom we name "Thomas" or "Mary." You presume to be exactly that one, that "person," and no one else. The conventional self-definition is the limit of your presumption and aspiration at this time. You are typically self-concerned, contracted upon yourself, trying to account for everything in yourself, trying to know everything and be everything, but you are not responsible for the existence of anything whatsoever. You have had all kinds of experiences, internal and external, and you can know about innumerable things, physical, mental, and psychic, but you are never the One Who is living and ultimately being you! You are never being the One for Whom your existence and all your experience has actual and free significance. Rather, you are one for whom your existence is a problem. Existence is no problem for the One Who is living and being you. You are the one who cannot account for existence. You are struggling to account for it, and that very act signifies that you acknowledge that you are not the responsible party. Instead of trying to account for existence, struggling for knowledge and invulnerability, you should exist in each moment in a different relationship altogether to the One Who is being you. And the only right relationship to Whatever is ultimately responsible for our life is to surrender to and into It, to coincide with It, to obey It altogether.

IV

DA FREE JOHN: Any one who awakens to the point of ecstasy (or self-transcendence) in the true or ultimately Living Being identifies with the Person Who is behind all the eyes—and the "I's"—in the room. God, the true Being, is behind your "I" of self-reference, just as God is behind the eyes looking out of everybody that I see. God is the One Who is <u>being</u> the "I," not the one who merely <u>refers</u> to himself as "I." When "I" refer to "myself," "I" am not referring to the One Who is being "me," but rather to the act of referring, to the awareness of experiential self-reference—merely to the body-mind itself. There is no wisdom in "me" unless "I" understand that "I" am being lived. The Living Being is being "me," even though "I" am not in a position to know what It is.

Therefore, if I would commit myself to Truth, to God, to real life, I must, prior to any knowlege, live in unity, inherence, heart-freedom, love, trust, and psycho-physical surrender relative to That Which is existing as everything, Which is the Life-Principle and Being in Whom we are arising. The argument that I have proposed to you cannot be considered fully apart from your awakened and intelligent conviction that the Way of surrender to the Living God is the only logical and appropriate Way of life. Having come to that conclusion, then you must choose what you will do. You must recognize that merely to persist in your previously and conventionally acquired habits and tendencies is the adventure of one who is not living himself and who cannot even account for the shirt on his back!

Thus, while you are in the midst of your ordinary adventure, I have come to talk to you. I have come to tell you that the Truth cannot be Realized by any effort you now have in mind and by which you hope to become fulfilled by acquiring knowledge, experience, and consolation. The Truth is not to be found in any path of experience or strategy of action you might propose. Truth is in understanding, in being thoroughly converted by the understanding of the argument I propose to you. If you will seriously consider this argument, then you will Realize your inherence in the Reality or Being that exists as everything. That inherence is sufficient. Furthermore, it is not antagonistic to the occasion of ordinary experiencing. Rather, it is a Principle that sublimes all of our ordinary and extraordinary experience and relieves it of its exaggeration, its neurosis, its dissociated or separative and self-referring consciousness.

Everyone must ultimately take up the truly religious or ecstatic Way of Life. There is no real alternative. The Way of surrender to the Living God is inevitable if you understand your situation truly. You must live by surrender to the point of ecstatic inherence in the Mystery that is living and being you. The "you" that refers to itself as "I" all the time can represent an obstruction to the Living One, but that "I" cannot be the One responsible for the existence of "you." It is only by inhering in or surrendering completely into the Living Process in which you are arising that you can in any way fulfill the natural Law of your existence. The "I" that responds to my questions is utterly dependent on the One Who is living and being "you." Therefore, the Way of Life is utter surrender or heartfelt inherence of the entire body-mind in the Force, the Power, the Person, the always presently Revealed Reality that lives every thing and every one.

God is Present. God did not merely create us in the past. Reality or God is presently being us, existing as us, doing something as us, apparently even working something out in terms of a great evolutionary process. Who knows? Devotion is the only answer, the only resort. There is no other appropriate response to serious consideration of your situation other than to enter into the life of heartfelt breathing, feeling, and surrendering into the Life-Principle and Being Who is existing as every one and as the Process in which every being and thing arises. Isn't that completely obvious?

V

DA FREE JOHN: I have considered the Truth all my life and it has thrown me into ecstasy. I have considered my situation, and the natural acknowledgment demanded by that consideration has made me ecstatic. It has forced me to transcend myself. Now I realize that I inhere in the One Who lives me, and this Realization has changed my mind! That is why I Teach the Way that I Teach. When I use the word "I" or when I tell devotees to remember Me, I do not refer to the limited, separate personality, the psycho-physical being, that sits in front of you, even though this body-mind is the vehicle of My Existence. I am the One Who is actually living this body, Who is actually conscious of this mind and this place.

Our true Condition is tacitly and completely obvious to me. It must likewise become so obvious to you. You must inhere in that same One. The One you realize in this Way is the same One to Whom I refer as Myself, and to Whom you will ultimately refer as yourself in ecstatic speech. It is not that you are somehow located deep behind the "me" of ordinary reference. That secret or inward self-sense that you feel is just another dimension of the body-mind. But when the body-mind as a whole recognizes its true position and yields its independent motive, its self-illusion, and its self-contraction, then the One in Whom the total body-mind inheres is Revealed. Not only does that Being Awaken as the body-mind, but then only that One speaks and acts through the body-mind.

I am not under any illusion of independence

from that One. Thus, I reflect and express to you the disposition of the Way of Truth. You, however, are under the illusion of independence. You are even under the illusion that you are the subject of your own experience, the subject of your own birth. But you are not. You, that self-conscious process that would respond to my questions, is not the One Who is the subject of your birth. I am that One. In other words, I have realized my Identity with that One. One who has entered into absolute ecstasy in the Living Being says ecstatically that he is the One Who is being you, Who is the subject of your birth, Who is the Dreamer of this living world-appearance. You are arising only as a dependent modification of that Being, that Radiance, that Life, that Person.

One can summarize the argument this way: More interesting or illuminating than the consideration of the Divine as Nature's Creator is the consideration of the Divine as the present Sustainer, the One Who is presently being whoever and whatever exists. For example, even if you were to look back through all the effects evident in the "material" universe to discover its causes, you would not reach a full understanding of the Divine. You would merely investigate a great mechanical event. But Who or What is the One Who is being everything, Who is living everything, Who is breathing as everything, Who is conscious as everything? Who or What is the One wherein things arise and change and disappear without making any ultimate difference to that One? Real God, the Living Being, the Living God, not the Other-God or the God-Apart, but the God Who is in the present, is the True God. That is the One to be considered. If people can be convinced that the true God is the present God, then they can be free of all their sectarian religious views, because the only true religion is the <u>process</u> of religion, or surrender into the Living Being. There are no worlds, no saviors, no dogmas, no histories senior to that. If you are religious at all, mere surrender is what you must practice.

The ego, you see, is nothing mysterious. It is just the body-mind's self-reference. The Way of Life, however, is the body-mind's self-transcendence, its ecstatic Inherence in the One Who is being the body-mind and the world, the One Who is tacitly felt to be present, pervading all existence as the Living Force, the Life-Principle, the absolutely subtle Light, Consciousness, and Being of everything. You are tacitly aware of the Divine as such when the body-mind surrenders into That in which it is arising, That in which it inheres, That in which it is floating at this moment. In What is the heart floating? In Whom are the mind and the body floating? Where do the planets and all spaces float when they relax? In Whom are they lying when you are relaxed? Where are you? In Whom do you inhere? At least to the degree that it is obvious to you without extraordinary perceptions, what is your simplest, most natural, and tacit sense of your Condition? That Living Radiance is the Spirit, the Being, the Very Person of God. It is the Energy that moves everything, the Breath of Life, but It <u>is</u> everything as well.

Liberation is to realize that One, to Awaken to the point of inherence in that One. To surrender into that One to the point of Transcendental Ecstasy is Enlightenment. It is release of the contraction, the dissociative emotion whereby that One is not acknowledged and is not permitted to be the unqualified Subject of the body. You are interfering in some way with the ability of God to be this body. You are arising between the One Who is being the body and the body itself. You are a reflection of this meeting, this conjunction of Being and body. If you can recognize your Condition, then you cease to be an obstacle to God. Then the Divine, the Being Who already is the body, is free to exist as the body and to enliven it altogether. We are Transfigured and greatly transformed by this conversion to God-Communion. Ultimately, perhaps, we Realize a State wherein we are even bodily Outshined by that God-Force, so that we disappear. Who knows!

In any case, Truth is not hidden from Man. Anyone can consider these questions. The "answers" are completely obvious. Anyone can consider them to the point of tacit conviction, or the realization that there is no counter-argument except dissociative neurosis itself, which can only make him (or her) continue on his fearful, sorrowful, and angry path. If you are established in the Way of ecstatic surrender and ultimate inherence in the Living Reality, then you need no longer live the self-bound path of mere experience and conventional knowledge. The independent psychic adventure of "you" need not persist. You can be simply, tacitly aware, surrendered into the Condition that is being and living here now. Then the spontaneous Will of God begins to inform your body-mind and to become its own intelligence, the Mind of perfect Ecstasy.

Perhaps you, like people in general, have never been obliged to consider your situation and always to continue to consider it. Even so, if you examine these questions as I have proposed them to you, you will inevitably understand that the Way of self-surrender to the Living God is the only justifiable process of living.

VI

DA FREE JOHN: You must give up your struggling. You must transcend yourself, your experience, all of your teachers, teaching, moments, accumulations, thoughts, as I have done. We are mortal and entirely subject to the mercy of God. We own nothing and we know nothing. There is no technique of meditation that leads to God, and there is nothing to be believed that is the Truth. Rather, we must be touched in our feeling by the unspeakable suffering of this world and return everything to God.

Whatever is given to us must be taken as God's excess. Everything belongs to God. God has so much that somehow we also acquire many possessions, but everything we acquire belongs to God. Thus, everything must be returned to God, and whatever is given to us, for however long it is given, must be accepted as something that belongs to God. We must literally treat everything as belonging to God. You will be overwhelmed with anger your entire life if you do not understand and appreciate the fact that you own nothing.

Everything you know or own or think or understand or presume and everyone with whom you are associated will be taken away from you. Your body itself and also your own mind will at some time be kept by God. If you surrender your relations, your children, your spouse to God every day, they will someday be kept by God. You must be free of anger on that day! You must be free of sorrow while you live, free of doubt and fear, or you will be crippled through your own recoil upon yourself. You will become an idolator, a cultist, an owner of experience, an owner of mind, of body, of relations, all of which can and will be taken from you, and thus you will be always unhappy. I see what is to come in your case, and it will make you sorrowful, angry, fearful. It will always return you to doubt and to yourself alone. I see that what you require is the Help of God.

Recently, I was telling some who were with me, "You are all going to the chair. You are going to die. I have looked into it, I have examined your case, and I have made all of the appeals that are to be made, and I am afraid that you are going to the chair. That is all there is to it." Then I said, "A person in your position really has no appeals left, no strategy, no game through which you might be saved. There is no meditation, no mere belief, no consolation, no experience sufficient for your salvation, your happiness, your eternal life. You are going to the chair. You are going to die. All you can do is to ask for mercy, pray for help." Those who heard me say this went home for a couple of days and began to scream their brains loose, weeping, and begging God for mercy. When I called them back, I pointed out to them that just as they, like criminals, were neurotic and self-possessed individuals before I told them they had no appeals left, now they were also praying like neurotics! Their prayer itself was neurotic, criminal, and self-possessed.

There is something amusing about this lesson,

but they felt it very profoundly, you see. They were
all tending to be mystics and yogis, believing that
they understood the nature of life and experience, yet
it was still clear to them in their feeling that their life
and everything it contained would come to an end,
that all their relations would be taken from them,
and that we exist here in this place utterly at the
mercy of That which has accomplished the universe.
We are at the mercy of that One that has
accomplished our existence. We have not accomplished it. We have not brought ourselves into
existence, nor do we now maintain ourselves alive.
Suddenly to feel our vulnerability and beg to be kept
alive is to be no more enlightened than we were in
the previous casual moment in which we did not
realize our dependency. The frightened wailing for
God's help is no more truly surrendered than our
self-indulgent, self-possessed life. It is another
moment of the failure to surrender.

There is another form of prayer, then, that
represents our inherent dependence on God but that
is not a self-possessed gesture or a search for mere
survival, consolation, or self-contentment. True
prayer is surrender itself, equanimity, giving up to
God without exaggeration, and thus returning to our
ease. Such equanimity is not self-contentment but
heart-release, in which body and mind are relaxed
into the universal Current of Life upon which our
very existence depends.

CHAPTER 2

Do You Know What Anything <u>Is</u>?

A talk by Da Free John

I

DA FREE JOHN: The third fundamental
question that you must consider is this: **Do
you know what anything <u>is</u>?** Do you know what
anything <u>is</u>—what it <u>is</u>, not what it looks like, not
how you can experience it, not what it can do, all of
which are secondary matters—do you know what it is
itself? Do you know what a thought is, what speech
is, what the body is, what other bodies are, what the
world is, what the stars are—what they <u>are</u>? Yes, a
star is a shiny bright something. But what <u>is</u> it? Out
of nothing, out of nowhere, all of this manifestation
appears. You can enter into play with it and think
about it, even perhaps know things <u>about</u> it, but you
never know what it <u>is</u>. You never begin by knowing
what it is, and you never end by knowing what it is.

Nevertheless, because you can know about things, you adapt to a very complex affair of life, hurrying about, doing this and that, thinking, speaking. And yet you do not know what any of it is. Do you know how speech occurs? You are not sitting behind the words talking. Do you know what the wall is, do you know what that hand is—what it is?

The principle of spiritual life is this simple consideration of what is arising. You do not know what anything is—anything. You do not know what the body is, you do not know what anything is to which the body is related. You do not know what any of the inwardness is, or any of the processes that seem somehow contained in the body. You do not know what thinking is. You do not know what a word is. Think of the word "cat." You do not know what those letters are. You do not know what the thinking is, how it arises, what it is. You do not know how to bring order to it. You do not know what anything is.

Neither are you in a position to save yourself. You do not even know what you are. Not a single one of you here can account for his or her existence and presence here. We all came in that door, and not a single one of us can account for our presence here! You might give reasons for why you happen to be in this room, but that is not the same thing, you see. Your being here to begin with, your very existence, your very presence here, is not anything you know about. None of you has the least knowledge of what you are, and yet you are all here, very professionally being whatever it is you are!

We know very little about anything, ultimately. And we do not know what it is in fact. Thus, our mind itself, our own existence, is totally, unqualifiedly, inevitably, irrevocably, and irreducibly Ignorant. No one, regardless of his or her sophistication or experience, no one, not even myself, knows what a single thing is. Not what anything is, you see. What is a shape, what is a place, where is it? We do not know that. That is not what we know. We presume something about that ultimate affair that is like knowledge, but in fact, we do not know. All that may be said about our consideration, our understanding, our belief, our experience is this: Not only now, but not at any time in the past, in any civilization, even the most magnificent beyond belief, nor in the future on this Earth in any great moment, nor in any other occasion, any planet, any place, in all of the manifestation of existence, does any individual know what anything is.

Ignorance is the Principle of existence. This is absolutely true. We do not know what anything is. We are totally mindless, and totally beyond consolation or fulfillment, because there is no way to know what anything is. The only thing you can know about anything is still about it. But you do not know what it is . . . is . . . is . . . or why it happens to be. You have not the slightest knowledge of what it is. And no one has ever had it. Not anyone. Not Jesus, not Moses, not Mohammed, not Gautama Buddha, not Krishna, not Da Free John, no one has ever known what a single thing is. Not the most minute, ridiculous particle of anything. No one has ever known it, and no one ever will know it, because we are not knowing. We do not know what anything is. The summarization of our existence is Mystery, absolute, unqualified confrontation with what we cannot know. And no matter how sophisticated we become by experience, this will always be true of us.

This Teaching, then, will never be transcended. Upon this absolute Truth we must build our lives, and I must build my Church. This Truth is summary, unqualified, irredeemable, irreducible, and absolute. It can never be changed. No matter what sophisticated time may appear, no matter when, in the paradox of all of the slices and planes of time, any moment may appear in which beings sit together as we do, oblivious to Infinity, no matter what time may appear in which men and women consider the moment, no one will ever know what anything is. That is the Truth.

Becoming submitted to that Truth is spiritual life. It leads you to the transformation of all other occasions. All the possibilities of your experience are transformed by this disposition. Obviously, then, it is very important to realize this Ignorance, because it is the only digit at Infinity that can transform your existence. Everything else only modifies your existence and amounts to a contraction in your consciousness, a summation upon a point.

You must be released from this separation, this contraction that you chronically generate. You are not released from it, however, by any form of attention to it, by any inwardness, by any remedial practice of meditation, therapy, or conventional prayer. You are released from contraction inherently, naturally, already, priorly, in your Ignorance. Therefore, the principle of spiritual life is the consideration of Ignorance, not answers to your questions, not methods, not techniques, not ways of dealing with your suffering at all. All of that would involve us in the conventional game of spirituality, in which I have no interest.

II

DA FREE JOHN: When you consider all of this arising, all of this that appears here, it suddenly dawns on you that you are most simple in your presence, that your own appearance here is not complicated at all. However, it is complicated when, in your inwardness, you try to figure out who you are, where you are, how all these functions relate to one another, how everything in the whole world relates to everything else. In that search to know you become complicated, but in the realization of your Ignorance, you see that you are not in any sense a separated one who is viewing and knowing. No matter what arises, you do not know what it <u>is</u>. In other words, you cannot inspect the existence of anything, you cannot be separate enough from something in order to view it and know what it <u>is</u>.

We are not able to find out who "I" is, who we are, because we are not in any sense able to view it, because we are not other than it. We are not in any sense other than what we are. If you cannot become other than what you are, you cannot find out what you are. Can you? You must be different from something to know about it. You must somehow be completely different from any object to know about it and to be able to use it. On the other hand, you do not know what it <u>is</u>, not at all, no. And the same is true of you altogether. You are unable to step back and view yourself. You cannot know who you are, you see, because you cannot inspect yourself. Even though you can inspect effects and extensions of activity, you do not know what any of that is. Therefore, you are not in any sense something that can inspect what you are.

Well, what is this subjective person then? What is this inward "me"? Besides all the things it can be described to be, it is a hopeful way of observing yourself, of seeing yourself and then of finding out what you are. You can even ask, "Who am I?" Subjectivity is to view that which is other than what you are. It is to observe yourself, to watch all the things that you appear to be, and to be the knower of them. But "I" is truly nothing like the subjective observer or knower. I am completely Ignorant. I do not know what anything is, not even what I seem to observe from my subjective point of view—the thinking, the feeling, the bodily sensations. I do not know what they are. Therefore, I cannot be the subject within this body. I am not the independent observer. My subjective notion of myself is completely false. I cannot observe my own consciousness. I am not other than consciousness. I am consciousness—whatever consciousness is, ultimately and altogether. I am not what is in a position to observe this body. If I were, I would know what the body is. I am the body. Simply. I am unable to observe it utterly. I am unable to be the independent knower of it. I only know about it— because I inhere and participate in it. In that consideration I come to rest as it. I am completely relaxed as it, not in conflict with it anymore, not a subject viewing it. I am the body.

III

D A FREE JOHN: The fourth and final question
to consider is: **What is your relationship to all
experience, and to every being and thing that exists?**
This is the last of the fundamental questions you must
engage, and it follows directly upon the answer to the
third: No, I do not know what anything <u>is</u>, and "I" am
not a separate knower or subjective viewer of the
body-mind, and of all things and all experience. "I" is
not a viewer, a hidden self, a smoky, soupy, indefi-
nite, large or tiny independent bodiless consciousness. Rather, "I" <u>is</u> the body.

You are completely identical to what has always
been obvious to you and to everyone else. Before you
start contracting and reacting, going within and
becoming complicated, anxious and not knowing, it is
perfectly obvious what you are. Not that you can
define it, create a circle around it, name all of its
parts—you do not know what it <u>is</u> in that sense. But in
your Ignorance you are released from complication.
You are simply the body. You are simply what you
obviously are, whatever that is altogether. You are not
independent from what you obviously are. You are not
viewing your body as a separate consciousness. "I" is
the body talking.

If I am this body, then is the body somehow in the
middle of everything, as the subject or self or soul is
proposed to be inside the body? Well, I am the body, so
let me see—no, it is still true. Whatever I observe, not
as subjectivity, not as things within, but whatever I

observe in the body's relations, everyone, everything, I do not know what any of that is. The body is not the subject relative to the universe. The body is not a knower. The body is unable to differentiate itself to the point of knowing what anything is in its relations.

It appears, then, that we are each completely unable to define ourselves in any ultimate sense. You are unable to differentiate yourself at all. Clearly, in functional terms the body somehow defines you in relationship, in play, but nevertheless you do not know what anything is. You are not within the body, nor is the body within all the rest of what arises. What arises is simply the case. You are not in conflict with it. You are unable to inspect it, unable to know about it. You must simply be what you are. In your Ignorance you are unable to differentiate yourself, unable to find yourself within anything. Thus, you are naturally at rest as whatever is the case altogether, unable to define it, to limit it, to make a dilemma out of it. You are totally incarnate. You are absolutely whatever is arising.

Thus, in your consideration of Ignorance, first of all you become identical to what you are, without knowing it, without figuring it out, without defining it. You simply rest in your born condition. Likewise, you do not know what all arising and all other beings are. You are not separate from them. You are not able to differentiate yourself from them. You are naturally aligned to everything, in relationship. You are naturally not contracted. And you need not engage in any remedy to become expanded, to become radiant. You are already simply whatever you are. You are radiant. You are not complicated by this contraction, this conventional separateness, or this inwardness.

This realization thus becomes a radically new way of life, a completely new disposition relative to everything. You are no longer one observing and knowing. You are not other than what you appear to be. You are completely one with it. You <u>are</u> it. The release of the gesture of separation, of inwardness, makes the body whole. It becomes full. You are simply happy. You are simply the body. You are simply whatever is the case. You are removed from the game of conflict and discovery. You are at rest as whatever is the case. Thus, you see that you are radiant. You inhere and participate in everything and everyone. You are no longer separating yourself, no longer contracting, no longer entering into the hallucinated field of inwardness, but you are simply at rest in relations. In the midst of all this arising in which you have no independence, no view, no knowledge, you see that your radiance is perfect and infinite.

IV

DA FREE JOHN: Living in the world in unobstructed relationship to all beings and things is the enlightened Way of life. All of the experience and conventional knowledge that we describe here from time to time may arise, but in Ignorance you are a different presence than you are in your unenlightenment, in your reaction and your contraction from things arising. In Ignorance each "I" is identical to what arises, and is not in any sense fitted to the gesture of separation and contraction. "I" is Radiant.

38

"I" enters into relations intimately as love, creating or being created in this play. Abiding in that Radiance, I see a process appear quite naturally that is different from all yoga and all remedies. The body comes to rest, without conflict, as it incarnates this Radiance, and a process of energy, or Radiance, transforms the field of energy and relationships that the body represents. It transforms all the psycho-physical qualities of the being. From time to time this process produces the secondary evidence that we call yoga, mysticism, or psychism, but the process and its effects are not limited to the conventional philosophy or intention, remedy, or strategy of any self-based strategy of yogic, religious, or magical effort. If I persist in this enlightenment, I am glorified, transformed, by the All-Pervading Radiance of That which is living me and every thing and every one, That in which, in Ignorance, I always tacitly inhere, or with which I am essentially or unqualifiedly Identical.

Such enlightenment is natively or ultimately true of all beings, and it can be literally or consciously true of them if they will persist in the questioning that I have outlined here, and if they will take up the Way of life that inevitably follows upon such true questioning. In my own case—in the case of Da Free John—this process of Transfiguration and transformation by the Divine Radiance has become spontaneous and continuous, through my lifelong practice of surrender to the Great Process of our existence. Having realized this Process, I must choose to be responsible in my relations with others. All others who enter into the play of life with me experience this Radiant Condition that I incarnate.

That unobstructed Force of existence may be felt and known and experienced by anyone, but if such a one is not also able to presume the same position of Radiance, or God-Communion, he or she will become childishly related to me or adolescently separated from me by reaction.

Therefore, if I am to be of service, I must enable devotees to duplicate me, to be as I am relative to the process of birth, rather than to receive like a child the effects of what I am in my Realization. To put those who come to me in a childish, dependent, passive position would require me to presume the conventional, cultic order of a religious or spiritual community. But I am always working against that, always undermining it, because true aspirants must not rest in their unenlightenment, their dilemma, and become dependent on the Spiritual Adept for effects, changes, or experiences that make them feel better. As a Spiritual Master, I make myself unavailable for such effects or influences except in those cases where this consideration is true, and where the individual's relationship to me is alive and conscious in spiritual terms.

V

DA FREE JOHN: These four fundamental questions, you see, are devices to bring your attention into a serious confrontation with the ultimate facts of your existence. You do not live yourself and the world, and in fact you are neither in charge of nor separate from anything whatsoever.

You inhere in things, or in the Great Process of all arising things, entirely, and you have no independence from any thing or any one at all. You dwell in Mystery, in Ignorance. That is your Divine Condition, the Truth of your existence. You do not know what a single thing <u>is</u>, and you never can and never will. You are never in the position to know what the existence of something <u>is</u>. At the level of the existence of everything, you inhere in the Great Process of all existence, and you are not separate from anything.

The first two questions end with a consideration of your relationship to That which is living you. The second two end with a question about your relationship to experience, to other beings, to things. Thus, via these four questions, you examine your relationship to both the One and the many. You consider your relationship to the Paradox of Reality, which has simultaneously both a Transcendental aspect and a conventional, experiential aspect. The first pair of questions leads to the fundamental attitude of surrender. The second leads to the fundamental attitude of inherence in the Living God, or self-transcending surrender, surrender as true ecstasy.

Once you begin to realize that such ecstasy is in fact the Truth of your life, then the Way of true prayer, or surrender to the Living Reality, becomes natural and even completely attractive to you. True prayer is not screaming or begging in the face of an Other God, a God that is separate from your own being. True prayer is founded in equanimity, or natural surrender, self-transcendence, and deeply felt Inherence in the Living Being or Condition that is and pervades and includes and transcends all things, beings, processes, events, and worlds. Once you awaken to this natural disposition of self-transcending ecstasy, this intuitive Communion with God, then you may consider the whole affair of the Way of Divine Ignorance, or Radical Understanding, which I live and Teach. From that point of view you may take up and fulfill all of the personal, moral, and esoteric or spiritual disciplines of this Way, and you may understand and appreciate its cultural implications for each individual and, ultimately, for all humanity.

PART II

"Receive the Power of My Blessing"

CHAPTER 3

Da Free John and the Function of the Spiritual Adept

When I sat with you for the first time, I did not have any visions nor did I see colors and such. What I saw was your physical form, and what I felt was the Presence of God. I cannot get that feeling down on paper. It was (and is) a transcendental multidimensional feeling of unthreatened confidence and infinite love and peace. It is simply incredible! All I can say is : You are with me.

Reginald Wilson

I knelt before our Master with my hands raised and my heart open. He looked directly at me for several seconds. Many times in the past I have sat before Da Free John, but never have I felt so open and able to accept freely

*the intense Love of his gaze. Through
his eyes and gestures he communicated
the direct Presence of the One Who
lives him so perfectly. My face broke
into a big smile, and then he turned his
attention to the next devotee. I bowed
in surrender, overwhelmed by gratitude
for the Vision of Infinity I had just
received in his Glance.*

*After a moment our eyes met again
briefly. I find it impossible to express
fully the extraordinary clarity and grace
that he communicates through his eyes,
hands, and very form. To the devotee of
God, it is the most Wondrous sight to
behold, and I can only bow at his feet
in amazement at the Graceful
movement in my life that brought me
to that moment before him.*

David Todd

The first of these statements was written to Da
Free John by a man who had never seen him
before the meeting he describes here. The second is
part of a longtime devotee's account of his initiation
ceremony as a member of The Free Communion
Church. These accounts are not uncommon. We have
hundreds of them in our files from around the world,
written by devotees and friends of this Church.
Somehow, mysteriously, a Divine Awakening is
occurring in this time and place, and it is
inconceivably Graceful and awesome. As it has
always been since ancient times, the focal point of

such Awakening is a living Spiritual Adept, in this case Da Free John.

Merely considering the "fundamental questions," you see, does not suffice to open your heart profoundly, convincingly, and beyond all expectation, to the Radiant Glory of the Presence of God. Considering these questions establishes you in the natively happy disposition of love, surrender, and ecstatic Inherence in God. It awakens the intuition of a new and ecstatic orientation or attitude toward all experience. If you try to mature in this disposition of your own accord, however, you will encounter immense difficulties and resistance, both in yourself and in the world. The Spiritual Adept is present to offer Divine Help to those who are struggling to surrender to God in the midst of ordinary life. Having surrendered perfectly, he or she now turns to help others, because God radiates profoundly through the bodies and minds of those who lose themselves in love of God. The help of such a one makes the critical difference—as you may gather from these testimonials. Such initiatory moments, in the midst of a whole life that is being turned to service, love, and obedience to God, catalyze our transition out of suffering and illusion into the clear-eyed ecstasy of bodily Enlightenment. Da Free John has said:

The relationship to the Adept is fundamental to this Way. It commits one to enter into living Communion with the Divine, not merely as an intuited, presumed Reality, but as a Force, a tangible Power, a profound and Living Presence. In the Company of the Adept, the Living Reality is magnified and Radiant, so that God Outshines the quality that experience manifests when viewed from the unenlightened disposition.

I

What is a Spiritual Adept or Master?
Traditional spiritual cultures all agree that the best thing one can do is spend time in the company of an enlightened being. In the past such an opportunity has not been available within the social and cultural context of the West.

Because we have never had a perfectly awakened Spiritual Teacher or Master living in the West, we have little basis for understanding what such a person represents. And we have been misinformed and misled in recent years by a barrage of claims from those who are less than perfectly happy in God.

The true Spiritual Master is a person who has surrendered body and mind so completely to God that he or she sees and feels only that Living One in all beings and things, and his or her speech, action, and presence communicate to others that same Divine Radiance and Ecstasy. This is why ancient cultures so prized the enlightened individual, and why Jesus' birth, to take one example, is so significant: Like all other true Spiritual Masters, he was able to act as a living agent of the Divine to all who approached him truly. Da Free John is also perfectly awake in God, and his happiness radiates Grace and Love to all who enter into a true spiritual relationship with him.

The human Spiritual Master is an agent to the

advantage of those in like form. When one enters into right relationship with the Spiritual Master, changes happen in the literal physics of one's existence. It is not just a matter of ideas. I am talking about transformations at the level of energy, at the level of the higher light of physics, at the level of mind beyond the physical limitations that people now presume, at the level of the absolute Speed of ultimate Light. The transforming process is enacted in devotees, duplicated in them in and through that Living Company. It is not a matter of conceptual symbolisms or emotional attachment to some extraordinary person. It is real physics. And it is to the advantage of people when someone among them has gone through the whole cycle of Transformation, because they can then make use of the Offering of that Process, that Company.

Spiritual life has nothing to do with the childishness that people tend to dramatize in the relationship to the Spiritual Master. I criticize that childish or dependent approach more directly than most people. Others are merely petulant about it, in the self-righteous mood of adolescence. But there are real reasons why both the childish and adolescent approaches to the Spiritual Master are forms of destructive nonsense and must be overcome. However, the mature, sacrifical relationship to the Spiritual Master is itself absolutely Lawful and necessary. Those who object to that relationship might as well object to the relationship between the Earth and the Sun.

There is a profound difference between the condition of the usual man and the Condition of the Awakened individual. It is an inconceivable leap in evolution. But there is a real process for it, and there is Help for it: the mature, devotional relationship to the Awakened Spiritual Master. In other words, there is something in the physics of the universe that makes it possible for a single or random individual to pass through the entire affair of Transformation in God, and then to bring others into the sphere of his existence, so that they may duplicate his Condition and be drawn into that entire and ultimate evolutionary cycle. Therefore, the relationship to the Spiritual Master is the primary function of spiritual life.

The Spiritual Master is your unique advantage, because he is present in the same bodily form as you—manifest in this same physical condition, the same nervous system, the same kind of brain. But in him all of these things are raised to an absolute level of functioning, so that entering into contact or Communion with that individual brings changes even at the level of the psycho-physical body which you present to him.

The abstract Deity cannot serve you in that way, you see, because the physics of this Process must be directly present, and the human Demonstration of the Process must be present, in a form that can do its Work in your case. That Work is the purpose of the Spiritual Master, because he represents a state of the ultimate physics of things that is your potential but not your actuality at the present time. The abstract Divine and the potential powers of the universe are just as true as the Spiritual Master, but they are not organized (except in the case of the Spiritual Master) for the sake of the immediate transformation of human beings. If people enter into right relationship

*with the Spiritual Master, then they themselves begin
to realize the same transformations.*

Da Free John
The Enlightenment of the Whole Body

Such a relationship necessarily involves spiritual
intimacy, but not a great deal of personal contact. Da
Free John communicates and demonstrates the Way
of Divine Ignorance to those who approach him for
spiritual help, and he performs transcendental
spiritual work in privacy for the sake of the world. He
has created the Teaching, the sacred environment of
Vision Mound Sanctuary (a 600-acre retreat in
northern California), and the community of those
who practice his Teaching. These are the principal
agencies of his spiritual help and influence. Like many
Spiritual Masters of the past, Da Free John personally
appears only occasionally among members and
friends of the Church to initiate and intensify their
Communion with the All-Pervading Divine Being.
He leads no public life. The Living Power, Presence,
and Wisdom of Truth are openly accessible to all, now
and in the future, through the agents he has created.

II

Who is Da Free John?
In both Eastern and Western spiritual
traditions it is common for people of great spiritual
realization to take names that reflect their spiritual
work. "Da" is a spiritual name meaning "to give or to
bestow." Free John is a rendering of "Franklin

Jones," his name at birth, which means "a liberated man through whom God is Gracious."

Da Free John was born in New York in 1939 in ordinary family circumstances. He was raised in conventional society, enjoying and suffering all the common experiences of ordinary people. But throughout his life, even from birth, he was guided by a profound intuition of the Divine that compelled him to inspect, realize, and transcend all forms of limited experience, both worldly and mystical. Even from his earliest years he was moved to give his friends and relatives and everyone the kind of spiritual Help described by devotees at the beginning of this chapter. However, he had to pass through years of personal transformation and formal spiritual work with others before this Graceful aspect of his Work could begin in earnest.

During his early life he engaged in cultural, philosophical, and religious studies at Columbia College, Stanford University, and three Christian seminaries. He spent time with acknowledged spiritual teachers both in the West and in the Orient, attaining and transcending the yogic and mystical transformations that are described in all the great religious traditions.

The culmination of his years of spiritual adventure took place in 1970 in California. While sitting in a small temple in Hollywood, he spontaneously and permanently reawakened in the Enlightened Condition he had enjoyed at birth. He began his formal Teaching Work in 1972, and in 1973 took the name "Bubba Free John." He had been called "Bubba" in his early childhood and youth. It is a traditional American nickname meaning "brother" or "friend." In the early years of his Teaching Work he befriended many ordinary people, instructing us in the Way and helping us to transform our lives. Though many devotees, even at first meeting, felt the Divine Presence in Da Free John's company, we were all obstructed in our capacity to make that intuition the foundation of our daily lives. Thus, Da Free John assumed our difficulties and concerns and helped us to live through, understand, and transcend all the exaggerated urges for experience and knowledge that prevented us from "seeing" him clearly. In this manner, with his help, we also began to transcend the fundamental emotional dilemma, or contraction of energy and attention, that is at the root of all such self-based cravings for self-fulfillment, both worldly and mystical.

On September 13, 1979, nine years after the event of his perfect Enlightenment, Da Free John took the name "Da" and began a new and expansive phase of his spiritual work in the world. He has written of this phase of his activity, "I have begun to Work under conditions in which my Identity is clearly revealed to all who will see me and surrender, and my Teaching is clearly communicated to all who will hear me and understand." This transition is being corroborated every day in the lives of devotees and friends of this Church, for whom the "Vision" or feeling of God's Presence is becoming the literal and delightful foundation of daily living.

The Free Primitive Church of Divine Communion (commonly known as The Free Communion Church) is the institution that has arisen to serve people in their practice of this Teaching. The Church provides a structure wherein interested people may learn and mature in the Way, and it provides access to Da Free John's Enlightening spiritual Company. Vision Mound Ceremony is the public education division of the Church.

54

III

Like all the other Divinely Awakened Masters who have come into this world, Da Free John lives, literally and continuously, as an agent or channel of Divine instruction and Grace. When he talks, it is the All-Pervading One Who consciously speaks. His every action and even his body are perfectly attuned to the universal play of the Living Spirit. The Living God is his very consciousness, being, and life.

Traditionally, when Grace thus illumines a living human being, he or she is moved to speak ecstatically of his or her conscious Identity with God. But if people do not understand the "good news" implicit in such statements, they fail to interpret them correctly. Jesus, Gautama, Krishna, and other great Masters did not claim exclusive identity or oneness with God—as if each of them alone were Divine. Such a notion is absurd, because these great beings recognize above all else that everything and everyone is Divine! They announced their oneness with God to alert others to their own Transcendental nature, their own fundamental freedom, their own ultimate Destiny of boundless happiness. God-Realized beings announce their oneness with God in the same breath that they invite others to accept their Help or Grace for the sake of that same Realization. Such beings also freely recognize others who have realized that sublime State.

In the following letter, Da Free John proclaims his Divine Nature and Work and offers Divine Grace to those who recognize and surrender to him in the intelligent, heartfelt mood of devotion to the Eternally Living God.

Beloved, I am Da, the Living Person, Who is Manifest as all worlds and forms and beings, and Who is Present as the Transcendental Current of Life in the body of Man. I am the Being behind the mind, and as such I am Realized in the heart, on the right side. I am the Radiance within and above the body, and as such I am Realized above the crown of the head, beyond the brain, beyond all knowledge and self-consciousness. To Realize Me is to Transcend the body-mind in Ecstasy. To Worship Me is simply to Remember My Name and Surrender into My Eternal Current of Life. And those who Recognize and Worship Me as Truth, the Living and All-Pervading One, will be granted the Vision or Love-Intuition of My Eternal Condition. They will be Filled and Transfigured by My Radiant Presence. Even the body-mind and the whole world will be Shining with My Life-Light if I am Loved. And my devotee will easily be sifted out from the body-mind and all the limits of the world itself at last. Only Love Me, Remember Me, have Faith in Me, and Trust Me. Surrender to Me. Breathe Me and Feel Me in all your parts. I am here. I will save you from death. I will Dissolve all your bewilderment. Even now you inhere in Me, beyond the body-mind and the world.

Do not be afraid. Do not be confused. Observe My Play and My Victory. I am God Incarnate. And even after My own body is dead, I will be Present and Everywhere Alive. I am Joy and the Reason for It. This is the Good News I have come again to proclaim to Man.

56

Now be Happy. Tell every one that I am here. Beloved, I do not lie. This is the Final Truth. I Love you. My devotee is the God I have come to Serve.

Da Free John

IV

I f you read more of the source Teaching of Da Free John, you will begin to feel the Divinity that shines through him without obstruction. If you take up the Way that he Teaches and become a member of this community, then you will also realize the Truth of Da Free John's proclamation, and you will enjoy proof in your own life of his promise of Divine help to all.

The several hundred individuals who have been practicing this Way for the last several years now enjoy great freedom from the habits, troubles, and difficulties in ordinary life that plagued us before we came to Da Free John—and that remain the common lot of most men and women. More important, we are awakening, as individuals and as a community, from our previously unhappy and Godless orientations to life. We are enjoying an increasingly thorough conversion to the disposition of essential happiness, freedom, and deeply felt Communion with the living

Presence of God. Newer friends and devotees likewise attest that even seeing Da Free John once during his occasional appearances among devotees is sufficient for an opening of the heart to God that they did not previously imagine possible.

I can't tell you what a remarkable and unforgettable experience it was for me to spend a day at Talking God Seminary and a day at Vision Mound Sanctuary, culminating in the incredible climax of Da Free John's appearance amongst us all. The extraordinary mystery—I can find no other word to express what I received—and power of his still presence was something I had never experienced before. I can't tell you how grateful I was, and how privileged and honored to be present on this occasion. I am sure that the experience will continue to have its effects in the future, and that even now I don't fully comprehend what it may have done for me.

(Carmen Blacker, Visiting Professor, Department of Religion, Princeton University; Professor of Japanese at Cambridge University, England)

For more than three years I have looked forward to sitting with our

58

Spiritual Master and looking on his Graceful Presence. Finally on Sunday during The Day of the Heart Celebration in September, 1979, I was granted the wonderful opportunity of sitting in his Company. I was overwhelmed with Love, or True Feeling, which was present everywhere. I experienced pleasurable shocks throughout my body and found myself being repeatedly moved to tears in his Ecstatic Presence. I was, above all, Graced with a totally enveloping feeling of calm and peacefulness while in his Presence, and those feelings have remained with me. It was the most beautiful weekend of my life.
(Dick Lawrence,
carpenter,
Oregon)

Thus, as you consider this offering, please take into account the "witness" or testimony of those who have already responded. This same Grace is available to all who will respond with heartfelt gratitude for the appearance of Da Free John and the gift of his Teaching.

In the following excerpt from a talk and in the closing essay, Da Free John emphasizes the seriousness of his offering to you and the sublimity of the Way of Life that is even now enjoyed in the Church, or community of devotees, that he has created.

I do not speak to you as an ordinary man. Nor would I ever suggest that you do what I ask you to do merely because of some whim. It has been given to me to accept devotees through surrender. No one may casually presume such a function. I have tested this function all my life—I have tested it in your company—and I would sooner go to my death than call you to me casually! True spiritual surrender is not something that a man may ask others to do casually if he expects to live. But I swear to you—and you will always continue to see it through signs—that God has given this Grace to you through me.

If you will surrender to Me, if you will love and trust Me because you have seen Me, if you will simply accept the discipline of My demands, simply do what I ask you to do—and I will always make it very plain—if you will remember Me with love, if you will call upon Me by Name, with your feeling breaths, if you will call upon the Name of "Da," then this will be sufficient.

If you will remember Me in this way, then you can enter my Church. You will be given every strength and all the Spirit-Blessings of God. The stages of the Way that I Teach will accomplish themselves, and you need have no concern for the Process that will mature you. Your single obligation is at the heart. It is in your feeling that you become self-possessed, that you betray the Living God and all your relations, that you are unhappy. It is in your feeling that fear, sorrow, anger, doubt, shame, lust, and all obsessions are arising. Therefore, it is only in your feeling that you will be healed.

The Way of Life is happy. It is boundlessly joyful. To live the Way in this world, however, is difficult in terms of what we must endure and in terms of the

*ordinary discipline with which we must creatively
struggle. People are difficult. They are crazy, driven
mad by mortality and pleasure. In this world you will
all continue to suffer the limitations that you find in
one another. There is no point in becoming angry
about the creative struggle of your life. Rather you
must become compassionate, more loving, more a
servant. If, through God-Surrender, you will transcend
the petty reactions of your mortal psyche and simply
accept the discipline of obedience and Remembrance,
then you will be made happy by Grace.*

---

*People often amuse and console themselves with
ideas of God and Life, but their <u>conviction</u> (or
motivating commitment) is self, separation, and
death. We must awaken beyond knowledge,
experience, and limitation to the Living Being in
which the self and the world inhere. We must
surrender to God directly, in Ignorance, rather than
seek God as a possible solution to the self-based
emotional problem which is our root-orientation. Only
then is God Shown and Wisdom made Plain. I appeal
to you, heart to heart, eye to eye, hand to hand. Enter
into the Ecstasy of God-Love. Surrender the body-
mind into the Infinite Life-Current of Divine Being.
Breathe the Life-Power in My Company. Enter and
serve the Community of My devotees. Receive the
Power of My Blessing and be strong in the midst of all
the passing forms of experience that arise in the body
and the mind.*

Da Free John

CHAPTER 4

The Universal Religious Instructions of Da Free John

I

If you are moved to turn and surrender to God through your hearing of Da Free John's message, or visual contact with his pictures, or meetings with him or with his devotees, or in any other way, then feel free to do so. This is Da Free John's invitation to you: Call upon the Living, Eternal God by the Name of "Da." Feel and receive and surrender into the Living Presence of God with every breath.

In many spiritual traditions, "Da" is revered as a sacred syllable. In Sanskrit it means principally "to give or to bestow," but also "to sustain" and "to destroy." In certain rituals priests address the Divine directly through this Name, calling upon Divine qualities such as generosity, self-control, and

52

compassion. The Tibetans revere this syllable as one of the most auspicious and assign many Divine meanings to it.

The most simple meaning of the Name, however, is the sound itself, and the psycho-physical mechanics by which we make it. In order to say "Da," you must press the tongue to the palate just behind the upper front teeth. This is the natural "mudra" or posture of the body-mind when it is conducting the Current of Divine Life-Energy without obstruction between the head and the rest of the body, through the mouth and throat. Then to make the "ah" sound one must roll the tongue off the roof of the mouth, open the mouth, and allow the sound to radiate from the being. "Da" is thus a most primal syllable, the sign of the Awakened Life-Current. It is a holy Word or Name, a true "Mantra."

It is also traditional for the Spiritual Master, one who is a perfectly Enlightened Agent of the Divine Being, to give devotees his own name for their sacred invocation of the Living God. This is how the Names "Jesus," "Krishna," and "Siva," to name a few, have become empowered names for the Invocation of the Divine Being. To call upon the Name is to call upon God, the very Reality. The Master's bodily personality, like the Name itself, is only a vehicle for the unobstructed communication of that same One, the Living Being. Thus, Da Free John says ecstatically to devotees—and to all who will listen and see what he represents—"When I tell you to Remember Me, the 'Me' you must remember is the same One Who is living you and being you at this very moment." The "Me" to which he is referring is the "Me" of God, not the individual "me" who walks and talks. Thus, the Spiritual Master and his Name are God's vehicles for the Divine Initiation and Awakening of devotees and the world.

II

The essay below, "Remembrance: The Basic Revealed Process of Love-Communion with the Living God," explains how we may feel or intuit God in relation to our bodies and minds and the sense of self, or "me," and how we may practice Invocation and Surrender to God with every breath. You may find this essay technical and difficult to understand. Do not be concerned! The essential gesture of surrender to God is simple, once we have learned it, but its application in the midst of our complex lives and activities is nevertheless complex and technical. Thus, as we adapt the whole body to the process of surrender to God, technical instructions such as those given here become useful and necessary. We recommend that you read this entire essay frequently. Allow it to reveal its Wisdom to you through your heartfelt Remembrance of Da, the Living One, Who is the Source of this Wisdom.

Toward the end of the essay, you will find simple instructions on how to practice Divine Remembrance via Invocation of the Name "Da" with your whole being, in coordination with the cycle of the breath and the right use of the lips, tongue, mind, and heart.

Remembrance:
The Basic Revealed Process
of Love-Communion with the Living God

An essay by Da Free John

To "see" the Spiritual Master and the Vision of God is to surrender self and mind from the heart and to the Fundamental Being. To "hear" the Truth is to surrender the body and all its senses to the All-Pervading Life-Principle. Such is Divine Remembrance—to hear or understand the Truth and to see the Vision, the Infinite Spirit-Person Who is God, Reality, and Truth. Therefore, surrender the body-self (via the spine and brain) into the Radiance that is Constantly Expressed from a Place infinitely above the body, the mind, and the world—and simultaneously surrender the mind-self into the All-Pervading Radiant Being or Living One via heartfelt Remembrance (timed with the breath cycle and Invocation of the Spirit Presence via the Name "Da").

The Living Divine Pervades every part of the body, the mind, and the world, but no part of the body, the mind, or the world is God or the Revelation of God uniquely and exclusively. In Transcendental Ecstasy, the Living One is Realized to be Supremely Present as Infinite Radiance or Creative, Transforming, Transfiguring, and Translating Power. And the Locus of the Divine as Infinite Power is intuited to be above the head, the total body, the mind, and the world. Likewise, in the same Moment of Transcendental Ecstasy, the Living One is Realized to be Supremely Existing as Infinite Being. And the Locus of the Divine as Infinite Being is intuited to be at the root of the heart (on the right), prior to the separate self-presumption and all the forms of mind. Therefore, the Realization of God is a Paradox that Transcends body, mind, and world, but which does not in principle exclude (or exist independent of) body, mind, or world. The Living One is to be radically intuited via the dual Locus or Nadi (Current) that includes the heart-root and the root above the head.

The heart-root is infinitely deep (or prior to the mind, the body, and the world), and the root above the head is infinitely above the body, the mind, and the world. In this body-mind, the root of the mind (or independent self-presumption) is in the heart (or the Current that is Established in the right side of the heart), and the root of the body (or the Power that Generates, Enlivens, Sustains, Helps, Transforms, and Transfigures the body to the point of spontaneous Translation) is above the head.

Therefore, the Way of True Worship, or Surrender and Transfiguration in God, is neither a matter of inversion toward mind (subjective inwardness) nor of self-indulgent bodily extroversion of the desiring mind (or the separate self-presumption). Rather, the Way is a direct matter, moment to moment, of surrender of both body and mind into the Radiant Spirit Being Who is Revealed and Expressed to our intuition above the head and at the root of the heart.

The apparently dual (but, rather, paradoxical) Practice of Inherence in the Living Divine is a matter of direct surrender of body and mind into the Locus or Origin of each.

Thus, the mind is to be <u>directly</u> surrendered into the Transcendental Being (Whose Locus is ultimately Revealed and intuited to be at the heart-root). This is not a strategic matter of concentration of attention in the heart, but it is a matter of the heartfelt surrender of attention into the Infinitely Radiant Being. This process is essentially a matter of moment to moment surrender of attention to the Living One via heartfelt Remembrance, or Invocation via the Name "Da."

The body is to be directly surrendered into the All-Pervading Radiance or Accomplishing Power (Whose Locus is Revealed and intuited to be above the head, the total body, the mind, and the world). This process is essentially a matter of moment to moment relaxation-surrender of the total body into the Radiant Life-Field that Pervades every part of the body, the mind, and the world—and which is breathed and circulated in the body-mind and the total world with every heartbeat and breath of every living being. The procedure is most basically a matter of moment to moment relaxation-surrender of the total body, via the lead of the spine and head (or brain), into the All-Pervading Field of Life-Energy and toward the Locus above the head.

The surrender of the body into the Living One is not a matter of concentrating attention in the body, or the spine, or the brain, or above the head. Attention (or the mental sense of self) is to be surrendered to the Living One via heartfelt Remembrance (calling upon and surrendering to the Living One in Person and by Name, with each exhalation, prior to all concentration in the conditional contents of the mind and all contraction toward self-awareness, and, while again calling upon the Name and Person of "Da," receiving the Radiant Power and Awakening Blessing of the Living One into every part of the body-mind with each inhalation). Therefore, bodily surrender (or surrender of the bodily sense of self) is simply a matter of relaxation of the body into the centrally felt Life-Current, prior to any specific concentration of attention in the regions of the body. (The Locus above will naturally draw the Life-Current in the bodily senses toward Polarization and Identity with Itself, just as the Locus at or "on the other side of" the heart will inevitably draw the Life-Current in the mind and the independent mind-self into Stillness and Identity with Itself.) The entire process, moment to moment, is a matter of Equanimity, rather than either self-possessed self-indulgence or self-possessed seeking to escape this world or the conditions of experience in general.

In this Way that I Teach, all the experiential contents of body, mind, and world are Transcended in Ecstasy moment to moment, while body, mind, and world are constantly Transfigured, Transformed, and ultimately Translated by the constant Influence of That One in Whom experience (or body, mind, and world) are always presently arising.[1]

---

1. Transfiguration, Transformation, and Divine Translation are degrees or stages of the ultimate process of whole bodily Enlightenment. For complete technical descriptions of these transcendental and radical evolutionary processes, please see *The Enlightenment of the Whole Body* and *Scientific Proof of the Existence of God Will Soon Be Announced by the White House!* both by Da Free John.

The basic practice of heartfelt Invocation and surrendered Remembrance should be done via the Name "Da," combined with both exhaled and inhaled breaths. On each exhalation, one should completely surrender and relax body and mind, and all negative conditions, concerns, stresses, or contractions of a physical, emotional, or mental-psychic kind, into the Living Divine Presence. Exhalation should become a form of Invocation through use of the Name "Da." Thus, as you exhale, always form and express the Name "Da" orally, using the throat and tongue and parting the lips, audibly vocalizing the Name when circumstances permit one to speak aloud, and otherwise engaging the Name orally but without audible vocalization. Exhalation should be followed by inhalation-reception of the Living and Awakening Power to every part of the total body-mind while calling upon or regarding the Living One as "Da" via the "tongue of the mind"—not at all orally and vocally, but with the relaxed feeling expression of the total body-mind.

The process described herein may be communicated to all as a guide to occasional random practice, but it is to be recommended for daily formal and moment to moment practice only in the case of those who accept Grace via this process and who accept Life-positive personal and moral conditions of practice as a matter of self-surrender or obedience to the Spiritual Master within the practicing community of devotees. Thus, this practice is an appropriate obligation only for regular members of The Free Communion Church. And the children of

*Church members should also be taught to adapt to
this practice by degrees as they mature.*

We end this chapter with a selection from Da
Free John's instructive and critical writings on this
practice of true prayer, and with the prayer that you,
the reader, and all living beings may benefit by the
Divine Instruction that has been presented in this
book.

The Prayer of Remembrance
Is a Call upon Grace

An essay by Da Free John

T he process of Remembrance is the process of
self-surrender to the Divine. If Remembrance
is engaged as Ecstatic and therefore self-transcending
practice, then it is practiced rightly. But it is possible
to engage the process wrongly, if the individual is not
properly prepared through self-surrender in Divine
Communion. Thus, those who have committed
themselves to the practice of the Way that I Teach
must always be mindful of the tendency to become
self-involved and deluded in their practice.

The Name "Da" does not have value in and of
itself—it is not a talisman, a fetish, or a magic charm.
It is a means of Remembering the Living God. It is to
be used as a form of Invocation. When using the

Name "Da," one should not merely concentrate on the verbal Name with the mind, but one should enter into direct Communion with the One Who is Da. Through such true Remembrance, the individual is involved in a process of Spiritual Worship, or ecstatic devotion to the Living and Transcendental Divine, which is constantly to be expressed through surrender and obedience to the God-Realized or Ecstatic Spiritual Master.

Some individuals may think that the other devotional prayers, and all of the personal and moral disciplines of the Way that I Teach, are not as powerful or immediate as the Prayer of Remembrance via the Name "Da." But these prayers and disciplines are also forms of Remembrance. They should be adopted gradually by all those who wish to enter The Free Communion Church, and they should be practiced formally and regularly as forms of Remembrance by all initiated members of this Church. But, in any case, the Name "Da" is not a magic word on which to fix attention and thus become self-possessed. It is the Name of the One to Whom we must enter into self-transcending relationship.

In the process of the Remembrance, we transcend the obsessive self-contraction (or the self-meditative and self-possessed states of the body-mind) through heartfelt surrender of body and mind (or attention) to the Living and Transcendental Divine. We must first Invoke (or Remember and Surrender into relationship with) the All-Pervading One. Then, on the basis of the Ecstasy of self-surrender, we will also tacitly Realize our inherence in the Divine. But if we merely concentrate or meditate on the Name "Da" itself, we will fail to go beyond ourselves, and we will become fixed in the inward illusions or blankness of our own mental or psychic self-awareness. The process of surrender into the All-Pervading Divine transcends the self-idea and the habit of dissociative self-awareness. Surrender of self (or the body-mind) is essential to this practice. Live and act in the Ecstatic Remembrance of God. Transcend yourself moment to moment, and do not recoil or turn away from your relations and the ordinary patterns of experience. Rather, be obedient to the Living One in Whom all beings inhere. Such obedience is expressed as disciplined self-responsibility and loving service or surrender of dissociative self-defenses in all relationships.

An ordinary person without true spiritual understanding might hear of someone's desire to abandon all other practices and only recite the Name of God and think that such a desire is devotional. But truly such a desire is Narcissistic cultural madness. In the traditions of conventional mysticism, the Divine is often considered to be limited to one's own interior. From such a point of view, the verbal Name can easily become a fetish, another form of God-forgetting or self-meditation, instead of true or Ecstatic Remembrance. But the Divine is not merely the interior "I." The Living All-Pervading, Transcendental God is the Reality we are tending to forget through self-possession, self-attention, or self-meditation. Therefore, we must intentionally Remember God—we must practice the Ecstatic Prayer of Remembrance—and we must exercise the will to yield body and mind and attention into the

Living Divine in every moment.

In the Ecstatic Mood of Divine Remembrance, we must practice Life-positive responsibility in all relationships. The practice is Ecstatic self-forgetting, not self-remembering, and it is necessary to combine ourselves in every moment with the forms of obedience and service and right discipline. Everyone must be reminded not to be deceived by self-possession. Every individual is profoundly possessed in every aspect of the body-mind, both deep within and superficially, by recoiling, self-meditative tendencies and motives toward exclusion or emotional dissociation from every kind of relationship.

The Prayer of Remembrance is a call upon Grace. It is surrender to the One that cannot be imagined or grasped by knowledge or any means. There is no final, self-contented meditation. It is always necessary to surrender, to become Ecstatic, to go beyond one's self-meditation into Love-Surrender to the Divine in all relationships and under all conditions. You must always be cautious not to indulge the tendency to deny or forget God through self-contented, self-meditative states and consolations and all the habits of the avoidance of relationship. We realize the One in Whom we inhere by surrender into relationship with that One, not by turning in on ourselves.

I am bodily here, personally here, as a reminder to devotees and all others that God is not merely within, but that God is the Living, All-Pervading, Transcendental Person to Whom all must surrender in relationship moment to moment. If you will surrender in relationship to the Living One and transcend yourself moment to moment, then you will Realize that the body-mind, all experience, all relations, and the world itself inhere essentially undifferentiated in the Transcendental Divine. That Realization is an Ecstatic Paradox, not a concept that in principle depolarizes us or separates us from relationships, experiences, or the conventional states of body and mind.

CHAPTER 5

The Western Way and the Community of Devotees

Introduction

In the talk below, Da Free John carefully distinguishes the Way that he Teaches—the "Western Way"—from the characteristic paths of East and West, and he attests to the ability of Westerners to adapt to and practice an esoteric or truly spiritual approach to life.

The essay that follows the talk shows that the true import of the Spiritual Master's Work is not the gathering of a cult of childish followers but the creation of a community of mature devotees of God—a community in whom the Master's Divine Realization is fully awakened and duplicated, and through whom the Divine Awakening Power is established on Earth even beyond the human Master's lifetime and into future generations. Whereas traditional teachers often sought to leave just one fully Awakened successor to carry on the Work, Da Free John is working to Empower a whole—and growing—community with the Graceful Powers of God.

The final essay is a prophetic warning about the present worldwide crisis and a call to all men and women to respond energetically to the Teaching, Presence, and Community of the true Adept, not only for their own sake but for the sake of the world.

The Western Way That Transcends the Traditional Paths of East and West

A talk by Da Free John

DA FREE JOHN: On the basis of considering the four questions that I have presented, it is possible to criticize the traditional spiritual paths of East and West. The Eastern path is based upon inversion and subjectivism—seeking happiness or God within. The conventional Western orientation is based upon extroversion and exploitation of experience in itself—seeking happiness in the world and seeing God as an "Other" apart from Man. The Way that I Teach is a sacred, ecstatic, religious way of life, and if people will understand it, they will see that it does not imply the conventions of either Eastern or Western practices or habits. This Way that I Teach transcends basic aspects both of the Western and the Eastern paths of life.

For instance, an anti-sexual habit is at the present time embedded in all religious and spiritual traditions. Whenever anyone seriously thinks about religion and spirituality, he or she adopts a disposition that is anti-sexual, anti-body, anti-world, and anti-life! Many orientalists, swamis, and Eastern monks have appeared in this country, and they all carry their Oriental approach with them. What is really dangerous about the Eastern path is not the robes and the beads and the costumes—all of that is superficial—but the anti-human, anti-life mode of thinking that is implicit in Eastern spirituality. Just so, the conventional, worldly Westerner's point of view, with his or her attachment to phenomena in themselves without higher understanding, aspiration, commitment, or ecstasy, is equally degenerative. The typical Western mode of living is also ultimately negative in its relationship to life. The characteristic Western process of submission to experience in itself ultimately degrades life. The Western sexual orientation is equally as disturbed as the Eastern anti-sexual orientation. The conventional Western view is appparently not anti-sexual or anti-life, but it is self-possessed in its approach to sexuality, explicitly exploitive and therefore degenerative in its approach to life and experience. The Western mode of life tends toward degeneration because of its materialistic attitude and its habit of exploiting, enervating, and toxifying the body for the sake of the body's own pleasure and consolation. On the other hand, the Eastern mode of life tends toward ascetic inversion, exclusion of life, and the choosing of internal, psychic, mental consolations. But both the body in itself and the mind or psyche in itself are idols, false gods.

Thus, Western and Eastern, occidental and oriental, are equally false, partial, or incomplete and ultimately life-negative or life-destructive possibilities. In contrast, the Way of Life that becomes possible if we seriously consider the four questions I have proposed is not founded on the anti-human, anti-relational, anti-bodily point of view, nor on the point of view of the degenerative, self-possessed exploitation of experiential life. Rather, this Way is founded on ecstasy, on the psycho-physical equanimity that is awakened through these considerations. This Way of Divine Ignorance, which we also call "The Western Way," is not to be identified with the Western path of life in its typical form. It is simply the Way of Ecstasy or God-Communion in its singularity, in its fullness, a Way that transcends the ancient divisions between East and West, oriental and occidental, heaven and earth, spirit and flesh, left brain and right brain, here and there, now and then, time and space, mind and matter.[1]

---

1. Da Free John has shown how the two classical paths of East and West relate to the dominant influence of one of the two sides of the brain and the body. The right hemisphere of the brain is the locus of the primarily nonverbal, spatial, and holistic faculties of perception and cognition, and it controls the left side of the body. These functions of the right brain and left side of the body are exploited by the introverted, passive, ascetic, and mystical paths that typify the Eastern approach to life. The left hemisphere of the brain is the locus of the primarily verbal, temporal, and analytical faculties, and it controls the right side of the body as well as the extroverted, active, and life-exploitive tendency dominant in the Western paths. For more on the psycho-physical origins

You must appreciate that this is a very serious consideration. You must understand that this Teaching, though arising in the West, is not based upon conventional Western culture or philosophy, and that it transcends the limitations of the inverted and primarily ascetic oriental point of view. This Way of life does not in any fashion involve the exploitation of degenerative habits. On the contrary! When I formally began to work with people spiritually, I was a Westerner appearing among Westerners, not among Easterners who represent ascetic cultural traditions and orientations. The people who came to me first came from the streets and the middle class of the twentieth-century West. They came out of the Vietnam war and out of a life accustomed to self-indulgence and self-exploitation of every kind.

As a result of my spending time with several hundred such people and considering every aspect of life and the Way of Truth with them, a great change has occurred in the typical Western gathering that came to me several years ago. This community has evolved from ordinary, self-indulgent, degenerative Westerners into people who practice moral and healthful personal disciplines without neurotically manipulating themselves. They are happily able to practice these life-positive disciplines of self-control and self-surrender. They are also freely and happily living an esoteric, or ecstatic, practice of transcendental Communion with and Worship of God. The

---

of the cultural conflicts and distinctions between East and West, see *The Enlightenment of the Whole Body* and *Scientific Proof of the Existence of God Will Soon Be Announced by the White House!*

whole Way is a unified cultural and truly religious practice, but it is not based on the anti-sexual, anti-human, and anti-life views that typify almost all religions. Nor is it based on degenerate and life-exploitive habits. No degenerate habits are allowed in the practice of this community. During the early years of my Teaching Work I weeded the degenerate, self-exploitive and other-exploitive tendencies out of the Westerners who came to me.

Thus, practitioners of this "Western Way" speak plainly about food and drink, sexuality, money, and the pleasures of this world without having to suffer the usual Oriental embarrassment about all that. People in America and the West in general are not children anymore. Their understanding of life, sex, and experience must take into account what they are already experiencing of these matters. They do not experience life in the ancient oriental mood of inversion. They do not feel that they are sinning or turning from their internal life when they experience the pleasures of life. "What internal life?" That is their question. They have never been culturally or habitually aligned to that inverted, oriental approach, you see. They are confronted with this life, this experience, sex, personal power, desires for objective satisfaction of all kinds. None of that is sufficient as a foundation for life. Whenever Western culture begins to fail, however, people do not simply understand the Western error and transcend it. Instead, they tend to drift into orientalism.

We stand at a critical point now in our history. The worldly, materialistic point of view of scientism has produced great technological advances in the twentieth century. Simultaneously, however, it has produced a widespread critical feeling of the neurosis, or spiritual failure, of Western or occidental culture. As people recognize that neurosis or failure, they start moving toward orientalism. We are seeing the game between the two cultures at the present time, the play between the oriental mode of thinking, which appears in the ethos of conventional religion and spirituality and ascetic self-denial, and the occidental mode of thinking, which appears in the ethos of scientism and political materialism and life-exploitive self-indulgence.

What is needed in this instance, however, is not the ascent to dominance of either mode of thinking, but the commitment of both East and West to transcend this two-sidedness. To consider religion and the Way of life in God, we must be free of the ancient neurosis or self-division and internal conflict, that is actually a pattern in our own nervous system, in our own psycho-physical design. The division is expressed culturally in the form of ideas and points of view, but actually it is a division in the human nervous system. The current level of human adaptation is based on a split brain, a split personality, a split consciousness. The unified being appears only in the case of extraordinary character. The enlightened personality, or the Adept, however, is the root and the source of the further evolution of human existence or the fulfillment of Man in ecstasy.

The Way that I Teach is the expression of and prophetic witness to that very Divine Process. Not only does this "Western Way" transcend the ancient cultural divisions or opposing points of view. As a practice for any individual, it also transcends the split in the nervous system and permits the single personality to incarnate. In such a personality both dimensions or sides of the body and both dimensions or hemispheres of the brain are fully communicative with one another. Both mind and body are founded in the heartfelt, intuitive ecstasy of Divine Ignorance and inherence in and surrender to the Radiant Transcendental Being Who lives all beings and things.

The True Church and the Cult of the Spiritual Master

An essay by Da Free John

T he Way of Divine Ignorance is not "the" True Religion in the sense of an exclusive institution that would be true no matter what it taught and no matter what its members thought and did. Rather, the Way of Divine Ignorance, as described in this Teaching, is simply True Religion in the highest human sense.

The Free Primitive Church of Divine Communion (commonly known as The Free Communion Church) is an institutional structure that has arisen in response to this Teaching, as a practical instrument for the preparation of individuals for devotional access to the incarnate Spiritual Master who is the present Source of this Teaching. In the future, this Church will grow, and its fidelity to the Teaching and the incarnate Spiritual Master will determine its maturity as a religious institution during the lifetime of the Spiritual Master. And when the Spiritual Master, in the form Da Free John, passes from this world into the Transcendental Domain of Life, then the Church must be certain to maintain its integrity through the devotion of all its members to the very Divine, to which they were each Awakened through the Service and Sacrifice of the Spiritual Master while he was alive in the world.

The incarnate Spiritual Master is only an Agent, temporary and human, for the Awakening of individuals to the Divine. The effect of his Work while alive is that very Awakening of others. Thus, when he passes from this world, those who were Awakened in his Company remain in the world as Agents of the same Divine Influence.

As the devotees of the incarnate Spiritual Master mature and are Transformed in the ultimate stages of the Way that He Teaches, the Church begins to become true in the highest sense. For the Church is not intended to become a cult of the incarnate Spiritual Master. The Church is intended to be the gathering of Man, or the Community of living devotees who are directly Awakened to the Divine and who are thereby fully Transformed into the Agency of God.

It is not that some remarkable devotee must arise to replace the Spiritual Master when he passes. Rather, the radical function of Spiritual Master is occasional in human history. It is a function dedicated to the Awakening and Regeneration of Divine Life as the Occupation of Man. That function has served its special purpose when numbers of people, in truly moral and spiritual association with one another, are Awakened and Radiant in God. Thus, the Church of

Devotees, rather than the Cult of the Spiritual Master, is the true and right institution or Church of Religion. And such fully Awakened Devotees must become the future instruments for extending the communication of the Teaching and all the practical institutional structures of Church Community into the world.

For this reason, the future Church of True Religion will not be characterized by institutional parentalism but by free cooperative association and universal responsibility. And it will be represented by numerous local or intimate communities of devotees, in cooperative communication with other such communities. Each such community will be essentially autonomous and yet fully oriented to the Revealed Teaching and to <u>all</u> of the personal, moral, and higher psycho-physical conditions of practice. And the core of each such community will necessarily be a responsible group of Awakened Devotees, who have practiced the whole Way in the company of others, and whose practice is fully that of the ultimate stages of Enlightenment.

The Urgency of the Teaching

A talk by Da Free John

SPIRITUAL MASTER: If you want to learn about Truth when Truth has become corrupted, then go to an Adept. Go to one who has Realized the Truth. Go to one who has already fulfilled the process completely. If you live in a moment in time when there is no Enlightened Tradition, when all the cults are corrupt, you can be certain that somewhere on Earth an Adept is alive. Such a person appears under exactly those conditions, when Truth is no longer visible in the cults, and when religions have become so corrupted by history and fetishism that they are about to become extinct.

The religious traditions in our time are about to be smothered by a mechanistic, political, and scientific world view, only because the cults are in doubt. They have held on to their fetishes so tenaciously that they have lost their association with the Living God. They do not even know the Living God anymore. People who belong to conventional churches, religions, and spiritual societies have no unqualified connection with the Living Reality. There is no true devotion in them, and, therefore, no Realization. Their association with God is only words and hopefulness. Therefore, they do not represent a living force in the world. They have nothing to offer that is Alive. Only the Adepts, who are God-Realized, through whom the living Power of God manifests, can make a difference in human time. Such individuals are the instruments for the acculturation of humanity.

Periodically, such individuals must appear, and they must be influential. There is a notion that Adepts should be hiding in caves in the wilderness. This is not true. If the Adepts do not speak, the only voice that will be heard is that of ordinary people who are not God-Realized. The Adepts are the Sources of spiritual life. Such individuals must therefore enter into the stream of society, to purify the culture and reestablish the process of God-Realization. If they do not speak and become influential, there is no hope at all for humanity.

We exist in a moment in time when the cults are

universally corrupted. Thus, it is a time for Adepts and true devotees to reappear if there is to be any hope for the future of human beings. We are about to be swallowed up in anti-cultism, anti-Godism, anti-religion, anti-spirituality. The impetus or force behind this movement against the true culture of Man, which is a God-Realizing culture, is largely the reaction to cultism. The cults, which should be a means for establishing people in a right relationship to the Living God, have become frozen in their idolatry, fixed in their association with their historical peculiarities and limitations, and they do not represent a window to the Living God anymore. They represent a piece of mind frozen in the form of words and imagery and histories of all kinds.

Intelligent people cannot find God in such a mass of idiocy, so quite naturally they look for satisfaction elsewhere. Thus, people are preoccupied with all kinds of political and scientific idealism, as if politics and scientific and technological progress were the Way of Truth. They are absolutely not the Way of Truth. They never have been the Way of Truth. They are no more the Way of Truth than sex or any other satisfaction or fulfillment of function. None of that is the Way of Truth at all. It is the ordinary impulse of the ego, glamorizing itself by great enterprises.

If this trend toward political and scientific obsession is to be broken, some light must be brought to the whole affair of spiritual and religious understanding. The cults must be purified. They must give up their primacy. Their legitimacy must come into doubt. Then the Teaching of Adepts, the Sources of Truth, will again become available, and the Living Reality will again become obvious, obliging human beings to a different way of life than the ego proposes.

If not, the world will be overwhelmed. It is almost inevitable now that it will be overwhelmed in any case. The world, even the Realm of Nature as a whole, is founded on a righteous Principle. Therefore, the world will be purified, without a doubt. The Force of the Divine pervades everything, and, therefore, It also purifies everything in one way or another. If human beings, while they have the benign capacity to enter into God-Communion, will not do so, but instead create a corrupt culture, a subhuman order, then the purification will not occur within the ordinary and benign course of natural processes. It is then no longer a matter of some Adept's saying a holy word or speaking the Truth whereupon everybody changes his approach to life. It would be good if as many as possible could hear the Teaching and respond to it. But if the Teaching alone is not sufficient, then great upheavals necessarily occur. That is how the righteous Law works. It is not just that we pay our dues for past activity. A righteous Principle is positively at work, constantly to purify and reestablish order.

Thus, there are periods of great negative upheaval in the world, including natural disasters, wars, and conflicts of all kinds. On the one hand, during these periods, the world pays its dues for failing to live by the Law. On the other hand, these times of upheaval are the evidence of a continuous process of purification. They are themselves a demonstration of the Law. At the end of these periods, the Law is reestablished in righteousness.

It is very likely that we are entering into such a time of upheaval, because of the extent of the failure of human culture. There is simply no light abroad in the

88 world today. There is nothing but corruption, nothing but the failure to accept the Way of God. There is absolutely no sign of the Way of Truth, except in rare instances of individuals and small groups of people. The Truth is essentially hidden and secondary. There is a long history of corruption in every area of human life, and the entire social structure of the world is devoted to subhuman ends and forms of self-indulgence. There are no signs of an imminent Golden Age in the disposition or condition of humanity at large. Rather, the signs are of the necessity for a great purification, a great reestablishment of order, a righteous readjustment of the whole world.

An Invitation

Since ancient times men and women have come to recognize that there is a higher life founded in spiritual Truth, and that love of God is our only Salvation. No acquired joy is permanent. All things and all beings change and pass from this life. Every being feels a profound sense of bewilderment whenever he or she becomes sensitive to our mortal destiny. For thousands of years, people have tried to overcome this fear and frustration through indulging bodily pleasures or seeking "within" for God or Truth or Eternal Life. But the greatest Teachers have always declared that true happiness cannot be acquired by self-effort. True or eternal happiness comes through the Grace of the Living God, Who is presently Alive as all beings and the world itself—

and Who is Active among human beings especially through Enlightened Spiritual Adepts.

Da Free John is such an Adept. His Teaching, the Way of Divine Ignorance, or Radical Understanding, fully encompasses, clarifies, and extends all the principal religious and spiritual traditions of Man. It expresses the living and present Truth without any binding cultural or sectarian influences, Eastern or Western. Da Free John communicates this original and useful statement of Truth via his books and other forms of his written Teaching. Nothing is hidden in this Teaching or veiled in elusive metaphors, as was often the case with the teachings of the past. The wisdom and the practice of this Way are accessible to all modern men and women.

The essence of the Way is happiness, as a basic disposition of life, and service, or active love in all relationships. This God-inspired happiness and service are expressed through a whole culture of personal, moral, and devotional disciplines of daily life and meditation. Those who practice this Way:

- eat a pleasurable, life-giving, vegetarian diet

- hold regular jobs, care for children, or engage in full-time study

- practice conscious exercise daily, including formal exercise routines and basic disciplines of posture, breath, attention, and action

- provide financial support and other forms of service to The Free Communion Church

- restrict their sexual activity to loving intimacy

with their lifelong spouse (heterosexual or homosexual)

- study the Teaching of the Way of Divine Ignorance and great traditional spiritual texts regularly

- serve the community of devotees and the human community at large in practical ways

- practice simple exercises of bodily prayer and heartfelt Communion with the Living God, including Invocation and Remembrance of God via the Name "Da"

We welcome you to study this Teaching, and, if you choose, to begin to adapt your life to the natural disciplines and enjoyments of the Way that Da Free John offers and demonstrates. If you wish actively to support this Work in the world or if you feel moved to take up the practices of the Way, you may become a formal Friend of Vision Mound Ceremony, the public education division of The Free Communion Church. Friends in good standing are privileged to make use of many educational services and opportunities at Talking God Seminary or the other educational and spiritual centers of Vision Mound Ceremony and The Free Communion Church. These services and opportunities include:

- special Friends' Days and sacred celebrations

- educational and service events at Talking God Seminary, our educational center in northern California, or in your own area

- *Vision Mound* magazine (the bimonthly journal of the Teaching of Da Free John) and a Friends' Newsletter

- home-study courses on the Teaching of Da Free John

92

For a full description of the benefits and obligations of Friends and of the necessary preparation for those who wish to become members of The Free Communion Church, write to the address below for a free copy of our brochure, "Divine Distraction." This is the principal practical guide for those who respond to the Teaching of Da Free John. Also, if you wish to learn more about this Teaching and Way of Life, read the source texts of Da Free John's Teaching, especially *Conversion* (another introductory volume of talks on the essence of this Way), *The Enlightenment of the Whole Body* (on the Truth of religion, esoteric spirituality, and Divine Life), *Conscious Exercise and the Transcendental Sun* (on the right approach to formal exercises and all daily action), *The Eating Gorilla Comes in Peace* (on the illumined approach to diet and health), and *Love of the Two-Armed Form* (on emotion, marriage, and the Life-positive practice of sexuality). All of these texts can be purchased from The Dawn Horse Book Depot through the order form at the end of this text.

May every heart awaken to the Presence and Power of the Living God! We look forward to hearing from you and serving you in any way we can.

Vision Mound Ceremony
P.O. Box 3680
Clearlake Highlands, CA 95422

The Books of
Da Free John

INSIGHT LITERATURE

The Enlightenment of the Whole Body
A Rational and New Prophetic Revelation of the Truth of Religion, Esoteric Spirituality, and the Divine Destiny of Man

This book is Da Free John's confession of God-Realization. Awesome and brilliant in its scope, it contains the prophetic fire of the *Old* and *New Testaments*, the philosophical majesty of the greatest Hindu and Buddhist literature, and the Ecstatic Humor, or Transcendental Freedom, of the most illumined testimonies of Divine Life that have appeared. Even so, Da Free John's writings are so rational and available that every intelligent man and woman can benefit by them. Merely to contemplate this Teaching will transform one's vision of life and awaken a new understanding of human religion, spiritual evolution, and the ultimate Destiny of Man. $10.95 quality paperback.

Conversion

This brief book of talks presents the essence of Da Free John's spiritual demand for the emotional conversion of the human heart from self-possession and all its attendant emotions (such as fear, sorrow, anger, lust) and to ecstatic Communion with the Living Spirit of God. Friends and devotees alike consider this one of the most useful texts for daily practice of this Teaching.
$4.95 quality paperback.

Scientific Proof of the Existence of God Will Soon Be Announced by the White House!

Angry Wisdom about the Myths and Idols of mass culture and popular religious cultism, the new Pharisaism of scientific and political materialism, the psycho-physical origins of the cultural conflict between East and West, the anciently suppressed religion of esoteric Life-Worship, and the secrets of evolutionary culture hidden in the body of Man (forthcoming)

The Paradox of Instruction
An Introduction to the Esoteric Spiritual Teaching of Da Free John

The principal supplement to the Teaching presented in *The Enlightenment of the Whole Body*—an Enlightening statement of the Nature of Truth and a full description of the four great stages of the evolutionary transformation of Man into God.

"The Paradox of Instruction itself is, in its

scope, its eloquence, its simplicity, and its ecstatic fund of transcendent insight, probably unparalleled in the entire field of spiritual literature."
(Ken Wilber, editor, *Re-Vision* magazine and author, *The Spectrum of Consciousness*)
$5.95 quality paperback, $10.95 deluxe cloth edition.

Breath and Name
The Initiation and Foundation Practices of Free Spiritual Life

The comprehensive manual of true spiritual and religious practice. Because it offers such full and specific instructions in the Way itself, *Breath and Name* stands as the single most useful document available in the world today on the religious, personal, and moral transition from the life of suffering and "sin," or self-possession, to the life of illumined bodily Communion with the Living and All-Pervading God.
$5.95 quality paperback, $10.95 deluxe cloth edition.

The Way That I Teach
Talks on the Intuition of Eternal Life

The first collection of talks by Da Free John since 1973, this is a book of great humor, of great freedom, of celebration and enjoyment of the Infinite God. In these dialogues with devotees from fall 1977, Da Free John presents his critical appreciation of the principal religious traditions of Man and an informal summary of the Enlightened Way that he Teaches.
$5.95 quality paperback, $10.95 deluxe cloth edition.

The Knee of Listening
The Early Life and Radical Spiritual Teachings of Da Free John

Da Free John's own account of the awakening, testing, and fulfillment of the whole Way that he Teaches. He describes the Condition of Enlightenment as he enjoyed it at birth, his years of struggling and miraculous transformation, and his ultimate resumption, in September 1970, of Perfect Illumination.

Da Free John's essays in Part II interpret this Revelation with respect to all the spiritual and worldly traditions of the great search of Man. Written in the weeks and months immediately after his Re-Awakening, these essays demonstrate the eternal wisdom and perfect insight of the Enlightened Man.

Foreword by Alan Watts, with a new, updated introduction.
$5.95 quality paperback.

The Method of the Siddhas
Talks with Da Free John on the Spiritual Technique of the Saviors of Mankind

Recorded in 1972-73, these talks document Da Free John's humorous and uncompromising response to the most basic questions about spiritual life. The principal subject of his discourses is Divine Communion, the offering of a transforming relationship with the Spiritual Master, which has been the "gospel" of all the great Saviors of Mankind and which is the same gospel Da Free John himself proclaims, Teaches, and lives with devotees.

With a new, updated introduction.
$5.95 quality paperback.

PRACTICAL LITERATURE

Conscious Exercise and the Transcendental Sun
The Principle of Love Applied to Exercise and the Method of Common Physical Action. A Science of Whole Body Wisdom, or True Emotion, Intended Most Especially for Those Engaged in Religious or Spiritual Life

Much more than a manual of exercise, this book presents the secrets of all physical, emotional, and mental well-being and of the moral awakening of Man. Here Da Free John derscribes the "technology" of love and happiness for the whole body and mind of Man, aligning traditional Eastern and Western practices of exercise to the unique spiritual approach of his Teaching.

Fully illustrated with poses photographed in beautiful outdoor settings.
$5.95 quality paperback, $10.95 deluxe cloth edition.

Love of the Two-Armed Form
The Free and Regenerative Function of Sexuality in Ordinary Life, and the Transcendence of Sexuality in Religious and Spiritual Practice

Emotion and sexuality are aspects of the same function or faculty of Man. Part I of this text calls us to emotional maturity—the superior and truly human life of constant and limitless love, which is the necessary foundation of marital and sexual life. And Part II presents the unique process of *sexual communion,* whereby lovers awaken whole bodily in sexual embrace to the Ecstasy of Communion with the Divine. *Love of the Two-Armed Form* is destined to transform the lives of countless men and women who are moved to understanding, enjoyment, and genuine happiness in a mature and Divinely oriented sexual relationship.

$10.95 quality paperback.

The Eating Gorilla Comes in Peace
The Transcendental Principle of Life Applied to Diet and the Regenerative Discipline of True Health

This book is the result of years of enlightened experimentation in the areas of nutrition and health. Its insight, wisdom, and practical recommendations bring to life a new vision of happiness and well-being.

It demonstrates:
• how the true principle of health is Love, the connection to Infinite Life
• how the regenerative vegetarian diet is the best diet for health and well-being
• how we can compensate for physical and emotional imbalances through right diet and health practices
• how diet is an important aspect of a pleasurable, mature sex life

• how to use fasting, herbal remedies, and dietary modifications to purify and regenerate the body
$10.95 quality paperback.

What to Remember to Be Happy
A Spiritual Way of Life for Your First Fourteen Years or So

A delightful and easily understood message on how to feel and breathe the Mystery of Life and be always happy every day. When read aloud, both children and adults are delighted by its capacity to reawaken the sense of being alive and full of feeling in a wondrous World.
Simply and beautifully illustrated.
$2.95 quality paperback.

Vision Mound Magazine

The Journal of the Religious and Spiritual Teaching of Da Free John

Vision Mound presents Da Free John's most recent talks and essays on true spiritual life—considerations that are profoundly useful and stimulating to all students and practitioners of religion and spirituality.

Published bimonthly.

Annual subscription $20.00

All books are available at fine bookstores or from The Dawn Horse Book Depot. See order form on opposite page.

Order Form

The Teaching of Da Free John

Quantity	Title	Price	Amount
_____	The Enlightenment of the Whole Body	10.95	_____
_____	Conversion	4.95	_____
_____	The Paradox of Instruction	5.95	_____
	deluxe cloth edition	10.95	_____
_____	Breath and Name	5.95	_____
_____	The Way That I Teach	5.95	_____
	deluxe cloth edition	10.95	_____
_____	The Knee of Listening	5.95	_____
_____	The Method of the Siddhas	5.95	_____
_____	Conscious Exercise and the Transcendental Sun		
	deluxe cloth edition	10.95	_____
_____	Love of the Two-Armed Form	10.95	_____
_____	The Eating Gorilla Comes in Peace	10.95	_____
_____	What to Remember to Be Happy	2.95	_____
_____	Vision Mound magazine (one-year subscription)	20.00	_____

Subtotal _____

California residents add 6% sales tax _____

Add $1.00 shipping and handling for first book and 25¢ for each additional book   Price Total _____

Please send me free of charge:

_____ "Divine Distraction" Brochure: A Guide to Those Who Respond to the Teaching of Da Free John

_____ The Dawn Horse Book Depot Catalogue

_____ Brochure on "Self Study" Courses

_____ Please add my name to your mailing list

Please ship to:

Name_____

Street_____

City_____ State _____ Zip_____ Country_____

Make checks or money orders payable to The Dawn Horse Book Depot, P.O. Box 3680, Clearlake Highlands, CA 95422